Hajar
Mother of Isma'il

A Story of Faith, Reliance,
And the Zamzam Well

Ibn Al-Akhdar Publishing House

Hajar
Mother of Isma'il

A Story of Faith, Reliance, And the Zamzam Well

Abu al-Hasan Malik al-Akhdar

First Edition: 1446 AH/2025 CE
Ibn Al-Akhdar Publishing House
ISBN: 979-8-89704-268-5
PO Box 8671 Turnersville, NJ 08012 U.S.A.
Electronic mail: editor@ibnakhdar.com

Cover Art by Ibn Al-Akhdar Publishing

Contents

M E C C A

Introduction

Several years ago, I was invited to lecture at a sisters' function in Newark, New Jersey. I chose to speak about the women scholars of Islam, as many are unaware of their rich tradition, beginning with the Mother of the Believers, Aishah. I also wanted to highlight some of the noble women mentioned in the Quran and the prophetic *Sunnah*, particularly Hajar, the mother of Isma'il.

Hajar's story is both powerful and inspiring. Left alone in a barren desert, she remained steadfast in her faith and placed her trust in Allah. Her resilience is a profound lesson for us—to rely solely on Allah in times of ease or hardship.

With that in mind, it is my honor to present to our sisters a short treatise that explores and clarifies the story of Hajar. This book includes commentary from *Al-Hafiz* Ibn Hajr and *Al-Allamah* Al-Sa'di and concludes with explanations from the two esteemed scholars, 'Abd Al-Aziz b. Baz and Muhammad b. Salih Al-'Uthaymin. It also includes the history of the Zamzam wellspring and the Ka'bah's construction. I pray this book serves as a source of benefit, reflection, and encouragement for our sisters, reminding them to remain steadfast and rely upon Allah alone.

Written by one in need of his Lord's pardon,

Abu al-Hasan Malik Al-Akhdar

30 Rajab 1446 AH

Camden, NJ

بِسْمِ اللهِ الرَّحْمَنِ الرَّحِيمِ

Hajar, Mother of Isma'il
A Story of Faith, Reliance, and the Zamzam Well

Arabic Text

عَنِ ابْنِ عَبَّاسٍ رَضِيَ اللهُ عَنْهُمَا قَالَ: أَوَّلُ مَا اتَّخَذَ النِّسَاءُ الْمِنْطَقَ مِنْ قِبَلِ أُمِّ إِسْمَاعِيل ، عَلَيْهِمَا السَّلَامُ اتَّخَذَتْ مِنْطَقًا لِيُعَفِّيَ أَثَرَهَا عَلَى سَارَةَ . جَاءَ إِبْرَاهِيمُ ﷺ بِأُمِّ إِسْمَاعِيلَ وَبِابْنِهَا إِسْمَاعِيلَ وَهِيَ تُرْضِعُهُ حَتَّى وَضَعَهَا عِنْدَ الْبَيْتِ عِنْدَ دَوْحَةٍ فَوْقَ زَمْزَمَ فِي أَعْلَى الْمَسْجِدِ، وَلَيْسَ بِمَكَّةَ يَوْمَئِذٍ أَحَدٌ وَلَيْسَ بِهَا مَاءٌ، فَوَضَعَهُمَا هُنَاكَ، وَوَضَعَ عِنْدَهُمَا جِرَابًا فِيهِ تَمْرٌ، وَسِقَاءً فِيهِ مَاءٌ. ثُمَّ قَفَّى إِبْرَاهِيمُ مُنْطَلِقًا، فَتَبِعَتْهُ أُمُّ إِسْمَاعِيلَ فَقَالَتْ: يَا إِبْرَاهِيمُ أَيْنَ تَذْهَبُ وَتَتْرُكُنَا بِهَذَا الْوَادِي الَّذِي لَيْسَ فِيهِ أَنِيسٌ وَلَا شَيْءٌ؟ فَقَالَتْ لَهُ ذَلِكَ مِرَارًا، وَجَعَلَ لَا يَلْتَفِتُ إِلَيْهَا، قَالَتْ لَهُ: آللهُ أَمَرَكَ بِهَذَا؟ قَالَ: نَعَمْ. قَالَتْ: إِذًا لَا يُضَيِّعُنَا، ثُمَّ رَجَعَتْ.

فَانْطَلَقَ إِبْرَاهِيمُ ﷺ، حَتَّى إِذَا كَانَ عِنْدَ الثَّنِيَّةِ حَيْثُ لَا يَرَوْنَهُ. اسْتَقْبَلَ وَجْهَهُ الْبَيْتَ، ثُمَّ دَعَا بِهَؤُلَاءِ الدَّعَوَاتِ، فَرَفَعَ يَدَيْهِ فَقَالَ: رَبَّنَا إِنِّي أَسْكَنْتُ مِنْ ذُرِّيَّتِي بِوَادٍ غَيْرِ ذِي زَرْعٍ حَتَّى بَلَغَ يَشْكُرُونَ [إبراهيم: 37]. وَجَعَلَتْ أُمُّ إِسْمَاعِيلَ تُرْضِعُ إِسْمَاعِيلَ، وَتَشْرَبُ مِنْ ذَلِكَ الْمَاءِ، حَتَّى إِذَا نَفِدَ مَا فِي السِّقَاءِ عَطِشَتْ وَعَطِشَ ابْنُهَا، وَجَعَلَتْ تَنْظُرُ إِلَيْهِ يَتَلَوَّى أَوْ قَالَ: يَتَلَبَّطُ فَانْطَلَقَتْ كَرَاهِيَةَ أَنْ تَنْظُرَ إِلَيْهِ، فَوَجَدَتِ الصَّفَا أَقْرَبَ جَبَلٍ فِي الْأَرْضِ يَلِيهَا، فَقَامَتْ عَلَيْهِ، ثُمَّ

استَقبَلَتِ الْوادِيَ تَنظُرُ هَل تَرَى أَحَدًا؟ فَلَم تَرَ أَحَدًا. فَهبَطَت مِنَ الصَّفا حَتَّى إِذَا بَلَغَتِ الْوادِيَ، رَفَعَت طَرَفَ دِرعِها، ثُمَّ سَعَت سَعيَ الْإِنسانِ الَجُهُود حَتَّى جاوَزَتِ الْوادِيَ، ثُمَّ أَتَتِ الْمَروَةَ، فَقامَت عَلَيها، فَنَظَرَت هَل تَرَى أَحَدًا؟ فَلَم تَرَ أَحَدًا، فَفَعَلَت ذَلِكَ سَبعَ مَرّاتٍ. قالَ ابنُ عَبّاسٍ رَضِيَ اللهُ عَنهُمَا: قالَ النَّبِيُّ ﷺ: فَذَلِكَ سَعيُ النّاسِ بَينَهُما. فَلَمّا أَشرَفَت عَلَى الْمَروَةِ سَمِعَت صَوتًا، فَقالَت: صَهٍ تُرِيدُ نَفسَها ثُمَّ تَسمَّعَت، فَسَمِعَت أَيضًا فَقالَت: قَد أَسمَعتَ إِن كانَ عِندَكَ غَواثٌ فأَغِث. فَإِذا هِيَ بِالمَلَكِ عِندَ مَوضِعِ زَمزَمَ، فَبَحَثَ بِعَقِبِهِ أَو قالَ بِجَناحِهِ حَتَّى ظَهَرَ الماءُ، فَجَعَلَت تُحَوِّضُهُ وَتَقُولُ بِيَدِها هَكَذَا، وَجَعَلَت تَغرُفُ الماءَ فِي سِقائِها وَهُوَ يَفُورُ بَعدَ مَا تَغرُفُ وَفِي رِوايَةٍ: بِقَدرِ مَا تَغرُفُ. قالَ ابنُ عَبّاسٍ رَضِيَ اللهُ عَنهُمَا: قالَ النَّبِيُّ ﷺ: رَحِمَ اللهُ أُمَّ إِسماعِيلَ لَو تَرَكَت زَمزَمَ أَو قالَ: لَو لَم تَغرُف مِنَ الماءِ، لَكانَت زَمزَمُ عَينًا مَعِينًا قالَ فَشَرِبَت، وَأَرضَعَت وَلَدَها. فَقالَ لَها المَلَكُ: لَا تَخافُوا الضَّيعَةَ فَإِنَّ هُهُنا بَيتًا لِلهِ يَبنِيهِ هَذَا الْغُلامُ وَأَبُوهُ، وإِنَّ اللهَ لَا يُضِيعُ أَهلَهُ، وَكانَ الْبَيتُ مُرتَفِعًا مِنَ الْأَرضِ كالرّابِيَةِ تَأْتِيهِ السُّيُولُ، فَتَأْخُذُ عَن يَمِينِهِ وَعَن شِمالِهِ. فَكانَت كَذَلِكَ حَتَّى مَرَّت بِهِم رُفقَةٌ مِن جُرهُمَ، أَو أَهلُ بَيتٍ مِن جُرهُمَ مُقبِلِينَ مِن طَرِيقِ كَداءَ، فَنَزَلُوا فِي أَسفَلِ مَكَّةَ، فَرَأَوا طائِرًا عائِفًا فَقالُوا: إِنَّ هَذا الطّائِرَ لَيَدُورُ عَلَى ماءٍ لَعَهدُنا بِهَذا الْوادِي وَما فِيهِ ماءٌ فَأَرسَلُوا جَرِيًّا أَو جَرِيَّينِ، فَإِذا هُم بِالماءِ، فَرَجَعُوا فَأَخبَرُوهم فَأَقبَلُوا، وَأُمُّ إِسماعِيلَ عِندَ الماءِ، فَقالُوا: أَتَأْذَنِينَ لَنا أَن نَزِلَ عِندَكِ؟

قَالَتْ: نَعَمْ، ولكِنْ لا حَقَّ لَكُم في الماءِ، قَالُوا: نَعَمْ. قال ابْنُ عَبَّاسٍ: قَالَ النَّبِيُّ ﷺ: فَأَلفى ذلكَ أُمَّ إسماعيلَ، وَهي تُحِبُّ الأُنسَ. فَنَزَلُوا، فَأَرْسَلُوا إلى أَهْلِيهِم فَنَزَلُوا مَعَهُم، حَتَّى إذا كَانُوا بِهَا أَهْلَ أَبياتٍ، وشَبَّ الغُلامُ وتَعَلَّم العَرَبِيَّةَ مِنْهُم وأَنْفَسَهُم وأَعجَبَهُمْ حِينَ شَبَّ، فَلَمَّا أَدرَكَ، زَوَّجُوهُ امْرأَةً مِنْهُم، ومَاتَتْ أُمُّ إسماعيلَ.فَجاءَ إبراهيمُ بَعْد ما تَزَوَّجَ إسماعيلُ يُطالِعُ تَرِكَتُه فلم يجِدْ إسْماعِيلَ، فَسَأَل امْرأَتَه عنه فَقالَتْ: خَرَج يَبْتَغي لَنا، وفي رِوايةٍ: يصِيدُ لَنا، ثُمَّ سأَلها عنْ عَيْشِهِمْ وهَيْئَتِهِم فَقَالَتْ: نَحْنُ بِشَرٍّ، نَحْنُ في ضِيقٍ وشِدَّةٍ، وشَكَتْ إِليْه، قال: فَإذَا جاءَ زَوْجُكِ، أَقْرئي عَلَيْه السَّلامَ، وقُولي لَهُ يُغَيِّر عتبةَ بابِه. فَلَمَّا جاءَ إسماعيلُ كَأَنَّه آنَسَ شَيْئًا فَقال: هَلْ جاءَكُم مِنْ أَحَدٍ؟ قَالَتْ: نَعَمْ، جاءَنَا شَيْخٌ كذا وكذا، فَسأَلَنا عَنْكَ، فَأَخْبَرْتُه، فَسأَلَني كَيفَ عَيْشُنا، فَأَخْبَرْتُه أَنّا في جَهْدٍ وشِدَّةٍ. قال: فَهَل أَوْصاكِ بِشَيْءٍ؟ قَالَتْ: نَعَمْ أَمَرَني أَقْرَأُ عَلَيْكَ السَّلام ويَقُولُ: عَيِّرْ عتبةَ بابِكَ. قال: ذاكَ أَبي وقَدْ أَمَرَني أَنْ أُفارِقَكِ، الْحَقي بِأَهْلِكِ. فَطَلَّقَها، وتَزَوَّجَ مِنْهُمْ أُخْرى. فَلبِث عَنْهُمْ إبراهيمُ ما شَاءَ الله ثُمَّ أَتاهم بَعْدُ، فَلَم يجِدْه، فَدخَل عَلى امْرأَتِه، فَسأَل عنْه. قَالَت: خَرَج يَبْتَغي لَنا. قال: كيْفَ أَنْتُم، وسأَلَها عن عَيْشِهِمْ وهَيْئَتِهِم فَقالَتْ: نَحْنُ بخَيْرٍ وسعةٍ وأَثْنَتْ على الله تَعالى، فَقال: مَا طَعامُكم؟ قَالَتْ: اللَّحْمُ. قال: فَما شَرابُكُم؟ قَالَتْ: الماءُ. قال: اللَّهُمَّ بارِكْ لَهُمْ في اللَّحْمِ والماءِ، قال النَّبِيُّ ﷺ: ولَمْ يكُنْ لَهُم يَوْمَئِذٍ حَبٌّ

وَلَو كَانَ لَهُم دَعَا لَهُم فِيه قَال: فَهُما لَا يَخْلُو عَلَيهِما أَحَدٌ بِغَير مَكَّة إِلَّا لَم مُوافِقاه.

وَفِي رِوايَة فَجاء فَقال: أَينَ إِسْماعِيل؟ فَقالَتِ امرَأَتُه: ذَهَبَ يَصِيدُ، فَقالَت امرَأَتُه: أَلا تَنزِلُ، فَتَطعم وتَشرَب؟ قَال: وَمَا طعامكم وَما شَرابُكم؟ قَالَت: طَعامنا اللَّحمُ، وشَرابُنا الماء. قَال: اللَّهُمَّ بارِك لَهُم فِي طعامهم وشَرابِهم، قَال: فَقَال أَبو القاسِم صَلَّى الله عَلَيه وسَلَّم" بَرِكَة دَعوة إِبراهِيم صَلَّى الله عَلَيه وسَلَّم "قَال: فَإِذا جاء زَوجُكِ، فأَقرِئي عَلَيه السَّلام وَمُرِيه يُثَبِّت عَتَبة بابه. فَلَمَّا جاء إِسْماعِيل، قَال: هَل أَتاكُم مِن أَحد؟ قَالَت: نَعَم، أَتانا شَيخٌ حَسَن الهَيئة وأَثنَت عَلَيه، فَسأَلَني عَنك، فَأَخبَرتُه، فَسأَلَني كَيف عَيشُنا فَأَخبَرتُه أَنا بِخَير. قَال: فَأَوصاكِ بِشَيء؟ قَالَت: نَعَم، يَقرأُ عَلَيك السَّلام، ويَأمُرُك أَن تُثَبِّت عَتَبة بابك. قَال: ذاكِ أَبي وأَنتِ العَتَبة أَمَرني أَن أُمسِكِك.

ثُمَّ لَبِث عَنهُم ما شَاء الله، ثُمَّ جاء بَعد ذلك وإِسْماعِيل يَبري نَبْلًا لَه تَحت دَوحة قَرِيبًا مِن زَمزَم، فَلَمَّا رَآه، قَام إِلَيه، فَصنع كَما يَصنَع الوالِد بِالوَلَد والوَلَد بِالوالِد، قَال: يا إِسْماعِيل إِنَّ الله أَمَرني بِأَمر، قَال: فَاصنَع ما أَمَرك رَبُّك؟ قَال: وُتعِيني، قَال: وأُعِينُك، قَال: فَإِنَّ الله أَمَرني أَن أَبني بَيْتًا هُهُنا، وأَشار إِلى أَكِمة مُرتَفِعة عَلى ما حَولها فَعِند ذلك رَفَع القواعِد مِنَ البَيت، فَجَعَل إِسْماعِيل يَأتي بِالحِجارة، وإِبراهِيم يَبني حَتَّى إِذا ارتَفَع البناء جاء بِهذا الحجر فَوَضَعَه لَه

فَقَامَ عَلَيْهِ، وَهُوَ يَبْنِي وَإِسْمَاعِيلُ يُنَاوِلُهُ الْحِجَارَةَ وَهُمَا يَقُولَانِ" رَّبَّنَا تَقَبَّلْ مِنَّا إِنَّكَ أَنتَ السَّمِيعُ الْعَلِيمُ."

وَفِي رِوَايَةٍ: إِنَّ إِبْرَاهِيمَ خَرَجَ بِإِسْمَاعِيلَ وَأُمِّ إِسْمَاعِيلَ، مَعَهُم شَنَّةٌ فِيهَا مَاءٌ، فَجَعَلَتْ أُمُّ إِسْمَاعِيلَ تَشْرَبُ مِنَ الشَّنَّةِ، فَيَدِرُّ لَبَنُهَا عَلَى صَبِيِّهَا حَتَّى قَدِمَ مَكَّةَ. فَوَضَعَهَا تَحْتَ دَوْحَةٍ، ثُمَّ رَجَعَ إِبْرَاهِيمُ إِلَى أَهْلِهِ، فَأَتْبَعَتْهُ أُمُّ إِسْمَاعِيلَ حَتَّى لَمَّا بَلَغُوا كَدَاءَ نَادَتْهُ مِنْ وَرَائِهِ: يَا إِبْرَاهِيمُ إِلَى مَنْ تَتْرُكُنَا؟ قَالَ: إِلَى اللَّهِ، قَالَتْ: رَضِيتُ بِاللَّهِ. فَرَجَعَتْ، وَجَعَلَتْ تَشْرَبُ مِنَ الشَّنَّةِ، وَيَدِرُّ لَبَنُهَا عَلَى صَبِيِّهَا حَتَّى لَمَّا فَنِيَ الْمَاءُ قَالَتْ: لَوْ ذَهَبْتُ، فَنَظَرْتُ لَعَلِّي أُحِسُّ أَحَدًا، قَالَ: فَذَهَبَتْ فَصَعِدَت الصَّفَا. فَنَظَرَتْ وَنَظَرَتْ هَلْ تُحِسُّ أَحَدًا، فَلَمْ تُحِسَّ أَحَدًا، فَلَمَّا بَلَغَتِ الْوَادِي، سَعَتْ، وَأَتَتِ الْمَرْوَةَ، وَفَعَلَتْ ذَلِكَ أَشْوَاطًا، ثُمَّ قَالَتْ: لَوْ ذَهَبْتُ فَنَظَرْتُ مَا فَعَلَ الصَّبِيُّ، فَذَهَبَتْ وَنَظَرَتْ، فَإِذَا هُوَ عَلَى حَالِهِ كَأَنَّهُ يَنْشَغُ لِلْمَوْتِ، فَلَمْ تُقِرَّهَا نَفْسُهَا. فَقَالَتْ: لَوْ ذَهَبْتُ، فَنَظَرْتُ لَعَلِّي أُحِسُّ أَحَدًا، فَذَهَبَتْ فَصَعِدَتِ الصَّفَا، فَنَظَرَتْ وَنَظَرَتْ، فَلَمْ تُحِسَّ أَحَدًا حَتَّى أَتَمَّتْ سَبْعًا، ثُمَّ قَالَتْ: لَوْ ذَهَبْتُ، فَنَظَرْتُ مَا فَعَلَ. فَإِذَا هِيَ بِصَوْتٍ. فَقَالَتْ: أَغِثْ إِنْ كَانَ عِنْدَكَ خَيْرٌ فَإِذَا جِبْرِيلُ ﷺ فَقَالَ بِعَقِبِهِ هَكَذَا، وَغَمَزَ بِعَقِبِهِ عَلَى الْأَرْضِ، فَانْبَثَقَ الْمَاءُ فَدَهِشَتْ أُمُّ إِسْمَاعِيلَ فَجَعَلَتْ تَحْفِنُ وَذَكَرَ الْحَدِيثَ بِطُولِهِ.

❧❧❧

The Story of Hajar and the Well of Zamzam

Ibn Abbas reported: The first women to use a waistband were inspired by the mother of Isma'il.[1] She used a waistband to erase her tracks and hide them from Sarah.[2] Ibrahim brought Hajar, the mother of Isma'il, along with her son while she was nursing him. He settled her near the House (the Ka'bah) by a [large] tree above [the site of the] Zamzam wellspring, at the highest place in the *masjid*.[3] At that time, no one lived in Makkah, and there was no water. [Ibrahim] placed them there and left them with a bag containing dates and a small waterskin. Then,

---

[1] This was because Sarah had given Hajar to Ibrahim, and Hajar became pregnant with Isma'il. When she gave birth to him, Sarah became jealous of her and vowed to cut her in pieces. So Hajar fashioned a waistband and tied it around her, then fled, dragging her garment behind her to erase her tracks so Sarah could not follow her. See Ibn Hajr, *Fath Al-Bari*, vol. 6 (Al-Shamilah), 100.

[2] Her name was Sarah bint Haran, Prophet Ibrahim's first wife and Prophet Ishaq's mother.

[3] Meaning the *masjid's* location, as it had not yet been built (*Fath Al-Bari* 6:101).

he turned to leave.[4] Hajar followed him, asking, O Ibrahim, where are you going, leaving us in this valley where there are no people and nothing [to sustain us]?" She repeated this several times, but he did not turn to her.[5] Then she asked, Has Allah commanded you to do this?" He replied, Yes." She said, Then He will not abandon us,"[6] and she returned.

Ibrahim continued walking until he reached a place where they could no longer see him. He turned his face toward the House (the Ka bah) and supplicated with these words, raising his hands,

﴿رَّبَّنَآ إِنِّى أَسْكَنتُ مِن ذُرِّيَّتِى بِوَادٍ غَيْرِ ذِى زَرْعٍ عِندَ بَيْتِكَ ٱلْمُحَرَّمِ رَبَّنَا لِيُقِيمُواْ ٱلصَّلَوٰةَ فَٱجْعَلْ أَفْـِٔدَةً مِّنَ ٱلنَّاسِ تَهْوِىٓ إِلَيْهِمْ وَٱرْزُقْهُم مِّنَ ٱلثَّمَرَٰتِ لَعَلَّهُمْ يَشْكُرُونَ﴾

---

[4] That is, he returned to the Levant. The narration of Ibn Ishaq states, Ibrahim returned to his family in the Levant and left Isma'il and his mother near the House i.e., the Ka'bah" (*Fath Al-Bari* 6:101).

[5] The narration of 'Umar b. Shabbah states, "She called out to him three times, and he answered her on the third. She then asked him, Who commanded you to do this? He replied, Allah'" (*Fath Al-Bari* 6:101).

[6] The narration of Ibrahim b. Nafi' from Kathir states, "She said, I am content with Allah'" (*Fath Al-Bari* 6:101).

Our Lord, I have settled some of my descendants in a barren valley near Your Sacred House,[7] our Lord, that they may establish prayer.[8] So, fill some hearts among men with love towards them[9] and provide for them from the fruits that they might be grateful"[10] (*Ibrahim*: 37).

Hajar began nursing Isma'il and drinking the water. When it ran out, she and her child became thirsty.[11] She started looking at her son as he writhed and rolled on the

---

[7] Al-Sa'di said, "Meaning: because the land of Makkah is not suitable for cultivation." See Abd Al-Rahman b. Nasir Al-Sa'di, *Al-Taysir Al-Karim Al-Rahman* (Al-Shamilah), 127.

[8] Al-Sa'di said, "Meaning: Make them believers in the Oneness of Allah and establishers of prayer, as establishing prayer is one of the most specific and best acts of worship in the religion. Whoever establishes prayer is upholding their faith" (*Tafsir Al-Sa'di* 127).

[9] Al-Sa'di said, "Allah answered his supplication and brought forth Muhammad ﷺ from the descendants of Isma'il. He called his descendants to the religion of Islam and the faith of their father, Ibrahim. They responded to his call and became establishers of prayer" (*Tafsir Al-Sa'di* 127).

[10] Al-Sa'di said, "Allah answered his supplication, and so fruits of all kinds were brought to it. You can see that in Makkah, at all times, fruits are abundant, and provisions flow to it from every direction" (*Tafsir Al-Sa'di* 127).

[11] In a narration, it states: Ismail was two years old at the time" (*Fath Al-Bari* 6:101).

ground in agony[12]. She disliked seeing him in this state,
so she went to the nearest mountain, which was Safa.[13]
She stood on it, facing the valley, looking to see if anyone
was there. She saw no one. She descended from Safa, and
when she reached the valley, she lifted the hem of her
garment and ran like an exhausted person[14] until she
crossed the valley. She then came to Marwah and stood
there, looking to see if anyone was there. She saw no one.
She repeated this seven times.[15]

---

[12] The meaning of يَتَلَبَّطُ is that he was writhing, rolling on the ground,
and striking it with his body. This is similar to the narration of Ata
b. Al-Sa ib: When Ismail became thirsty, he began striking the
ground with his heels." In the narration of Ibrahim b. Nafi', it states,
 It was as if he was gasping for life," meaning he was heaving, his
voice rising and falling, like someone in the throes of death. See *Fath
Al-Bari* 6:101.

[13] In the narration of 'Ata b. Al-Sa'ib, it states, At that time, the
valley was deep." In the *hadith* of Abu Jahm, it states, She was
seeking help from her Lord and supplicating to Him" (*Fath Al-Bari*
6:10).

[14] Meaning: the one who was afflicted by hardship, which refers to a
difficult and exhausting situation. See *Fath Al-Bari* 6:10.

[15] The phrase "seven times" in the hadith of Abu Jahm refers to the
first instance of *Sa'i* (running) between Safa and Marwah. In the
narration of Ibrahim b. Nafi , it is stated, Each time, she would
check on Isma'il and see what had happened to him." In his
narration, it is also mentioned, Her soul did not let her remain

Ibn Abbas said, "The Prophet ﷺ stated, 'This is the origin of the *Sa i* (the running) between Safa and Marwah.'"

When Hajar reached Marwah on her last lap, she heard a voice. She said, Quiet,"[16] intending to listen carefully. She heard the voice again and said, You have made me hear you. If you can help us, then do so."[17] She found an angel (Jibril) at the location of Zamzam, digging into the

---

calm," meaning she could not stay still, watching him die, so she returned. This refers to the final lap. See *Fath Al-Bari* 6:101.

[16] It seems she was addressing herself, telling herself to stay silent. In the narration of Ibrahim b. Nafi' and Ibn Jurayj, it is mentioned, She said, Help me if you have any goodness with you'" (*Fath Al-Bari* 6:102).

[17] In the narration of Ibrahim b. Nafi' and Ibn Jurayj, it states, And it was Jibril." In the hadith of Ali, recorded by al-Tabari with a sound chain of transmission, it is mentioned, Jibril called out to her and said, Who are you?' She replied, I am Hajar, the mother of Ibrahim s child. He said, To whom has he entrusted you?' She replied, To Allah.' He said, He has entrusted you to the One who is sufficient'" (*Fath Al-Bari* 6:102).

earth with either his heel or wing[18] until water appeared.[19] She began collecting the water and forming a basin around it with her hands.[20] She scooped water into her waterskin, and the water kept flowing after she scooped it.

The Prophet ﷺ said, May Allah have mercy on the mother of Isma'il. Had she left Zamzam alone or not scooped from the water, Zamzam would have been a

---

[18] The narrator expressed doubt [about the exact wording]. In the narration of Ibrahim b. Nafi , it states, He struck the ground with his heel like this and pressed his heel into the earth," which confirms that it was done with his heel. In the narration of Ibn Jurayj, it states, "Jibril struck the ground with his foot." In the hadith of Ali, it states, He dug into the ground with his finger, and Zamzam gushed forth." Ibn Ishaq mentioned in his narration, The scholars have long stated that this was the strike of Jibril's heel." (*Fath Al-Bari* 6:102).

[19] In the narration of Ibn Jurayj, it states, The water flowed abundantly." The narration of Ibn Nafi' states, The water gushed forth." The word انبثق indicates that it burst forth. See *Fath Al-Bari* 6:102.

[20] Meaning: she shaped it like a basin. In the narration of Ibn Nafi , it states, The mother of Isma'il was astonished and began digging" (*Fath Al-Bari* 6:102).

flowing spring."²¹ He ﷺ added, "She drank the water and nursed her child."

The angel told her, "Do not fear abandonment,²² for here is a house of Allah that this boy and his father will build, and Allah does not abandon His people." At that time, the House was a mound of earth raised above ground level, and floods would pass by it to its right and left.²³

---

²¹ Meaning: flowing visibly on the surface of the earth. See *Fath Al-Bari* 6:102.

²² In the *hadith* of Abu Jahm, it states, "Do not fear that the water will run out." In the narration of Ali b. al-Wazi' from Ayyub, as recorded by Al-Fakihi, it states, "Do not worry about the people of this valley suffering from thirst, for this is a spring from which Allah s guests will drink" (*Fath Al-Bari* 6:102).

²³ Ibn Abi Hatim narrated from 'Abd Allah b. Amr b. al-As who said, "During the time of the Flood, the House was lifted, and the prophets would perform Hajj to it without knowing its exact location until Allah guided Ibrahim there and showed him its location."

Al-Bayhaqi narrated in *Dala il Al-Nubuwwah* through another chain from Abd Allah b. Amr as a *marfu'* narration, "Allah sent Jibril to Adam and commanded him to build the House. Adam built it and was then commanded to perform *tawaf* around it. He was told, 'You are the first of mankind, and this is the first House established for mankind.'"

Hajar lived in this condition until a group of travelers from the tribe of Jurhum[24] passed by her, coming through the route of Kada . They saw a bird circling[25] and said, This bird must be near water, though we are not accustomed to water being in this valley." They sent a scout and found the wellspring. They returned and informed their group, who came to Hajar and asked, Do

---

Abd Al-Razzaq narrated from Ibn Jurayj, from Ata, Adam was the first to build the House," while others said, The angels built it before him."

Wahb b. Munabbih said, The first to build it was Shith, the son of Adam."

However, the first opinion is more firmly established. See *Fath Al-Bari* 6:102-103.

[24] Jurhum is the son of Qahtan, son of 'Amir, son of Shalikh, son of Arfakhshad, son of Sam, son of Nuh. Some narrations suggest he is the son of Yaqtun. Ibn Ishaq stated, Jurhum and his brother Qatura were the first to speak Arabic after the tongues were diversified. The leader of Jurhum was Midad b. 'Amr, and the leader of Qatura was Al-Samayda . Both groups were collectively referred to as Jurhum."

According to the narration of Ata b. al-Sa ib, Jurhum, at that time, resided in a valley near Makkah." It is also said that their origins trace back to the Amalekites. See *Fath Al-Bari* 6:103.

[25] It refers to birds that circle above water, hover over it, and do not move away from it. See *Fath Al-Bari* 6:103.

you permit us to settle here?" She replied, Yes, but you have no right to the water." They agreed.

Ibn Abbas said, the Prophet ﷺ said, Hajar loved the company of people, so they settled there and sent for their families to join them."

The child (i.e., Isma'il) grew up,[26] learned Arabic from them,[27] and became one of them. They married him to a

---

[26] In the *hadith* of Abu Jahm, it states, Isma'il grew up among their children" (*Fath Al-Bari* 6:103).

[27] This indicates that the language of Isma'il s mother and father was not Arabic, and it weakens the claim of those who narrate that he was the first to speak Arabic. This claim appears in a *hadith* of Ibn Abbas, recorded by Al-Hakim in Al-Mustadrak, with the wording, The first to speak Arabic was Ismail." Al-Zubayr b. Bakkar also narrated in *Al-Nasab*, with a sound chain of narration from Ali, who said, The first person Allah blessed to speak eloquent Arabic was Isma'il."

With this clarification, the two narrations align: Ismail's precedence in Arabic means he was the first to speak it clearly and eloquently, not the first overall. This suggests that after learning the foundations of Arabic from Jurhum, Allah inspired him with eloquent and articulate Arabic, which he then spoke.

This is supported by what Ibn Hisham narrated from Al-Sharqi b. Qutami, The Arabic of Ismail was more eloquent than that of Ya rub b. Qahtan, the remnants of Himyar and Jurhum."

woman from among them when he reached maturity. Hajar passed away.

It is also possible that the precedence mentioned in the *hadith* is relative to Isma'il s siblings from the descendants of Ibrahim. Thus, Isma'il would be the first among Ibrahim s descendants to speak Arabic. See *Fath Al-Bari* 6:103.

Ibrahim later visited and found Isma'il s wife at home, but not Isma il.[28] He asked her about their condition, and she complained of hardship and poverty. Ibrahim said to her, When your husband returns, convey my greetings to him and tell him to change the threshold of his door."[29] When Isma'il returned, and she informed him, he said, That was my father, and he has instructed me to separate from you." He divorced her and married another woman.

Time passed, and Ibrahim returned. Again, he did not find Isma il at home and asked his new wife about their condition. She praised Allah and spoke of their good state. Ibrahim said, When your husband returns, convey my greetings to him and tell him to keep the threshold of his door firm." When Isma il returned, she relayed the message. He said, That was my father, and you are the

---

[28] In the narration of Ata b. al-Sa ib, it states: Ibrahim returned to find that Hajar had passed away" (*Fath Al-Bari* 6:104).

[29] This metaphor refers to women. They are described as the threshold" because they safeguard the household, protect what is within, and serve as the foundation of marital intimacy. Thus, changing the threshold" can mean divorcing them. See *Fath Al-Bari* 6:104.

threshold of my door. He has instructed me to keep you."[30]

Ibrahim returned again to find Isma'il sharpening arrows under a tree near Zamzam. They greeted each other warmly. Ibrahim said, O Isma il, Allah has commanded me to build a house here."

Obey your Lord," Ismail said.

Will you help me?"

I will."

They began building the Ka'bah, with Isma'il bringing the stones and Ibrahim constructing the walls. When the walls became high, Ibrahim stood on a stone (the Maqam of Ibrahim) while Ismail handed him rocks. They continued building, saying,

---

[30] Prophet Ibrahim's advice came because Isma'il's wife neither thanked Allah for His blessings nor appreciated her husband's kindness. Following his father's advice, Isma'il divorced her and married another woman. When Ibrahim later visited and asked the second wife about their situation, she expressed gratitude to Allah and appreciation for her husband. Pleased with her response, he instructed Isma'il to remain with her. This shows the importance of gratitude, as a grateful spouse creates a happy and stable house.

Our Lord, accept this from us. Indeed, You are the Hearing, the Knowing" (*Al-Baqarah*: 2:127).[31]

In another wording of the narration, Ibrahim set out with Isma'il and Isma'il's mother, carrying a waterskin with some water. Isma'il's mother would drink from it, and her milk would flow to nourish her infant until they reached Makkah. Ibrahim placed her under a tree there, then returned to his people. Isma'il's mother followed him until they reached Kada', where she called out to him, "O Ibrahim, to whom are you leaving us?" He replied, "To Allah." She said, "I am content with Him." Then she returned and continued drinking from the waterskin, and her milk flowed for her child.

When the water ran out, she said, "If I look, perhaps I will find someone." So she went up to Safa, looked around, and searched for anyone, but saw no one. When she reached the valley, she ran, then went to Marwah and did the same, completing several passes. Then she said, "Let me go back and check on the child." When she

---

[31] This *hadith* is collected by Al-Bukhari in his *Sahih* (no. 3184).

returned, she found him as he had been, gasping as if on the verge of death, and she could not bear it.

She said, "If I look again, perhaps I will find someone." She climbed Safa once more, looking and searching, but found no one until she had completed seven passes. Then she said, "Let me go back and check on him."
Suddenly, she heard a voice and called out, "Help us if you have anything good!" And there was Jibril. He struck the ground with his heel like this—the narrator gestured—and water gushed forth. Isma'il's mother was astonished and began scooping it up.

Explanation of Al-Allamah Abd Al-Aziz b. Baz

Al-Allamah 'Abd Al-Aziz b. Baz said, "This *hadith* recounts the story of Ibrahim's migration with Hajar, the mother of Isma'il, to Makkah. Hajar was a bondwoman given to him by the king of Egypt. Ibrahim had a son, Isma'il, with her. He brought them from the Levant to Makkah and left them there by Allah s command, near the site of the Ka'bah, with her young son. Alongside them, he left a bag of dates and a waterskin by Allah s order, and then he departed.

Hajar asked him, 'How can you leave us here?' She then asked, 'Did Allah command you to do this?' He replied, 'Yes.' She said, 'Then He will not abandon us.' By this, she meant that as long as it was Allah s command, He would not forsake His servants and allies. She stayed with her son, drinking the water and eating the dates.

When the water ran out, she searched for help, hoping to find someone.[32] She climbed Mount Safa, then Mount Marwah, seeking people, running between them seven times. Finally, she heard a voice. She said, 'If you can help us, then do so.' It was the voice of Jibril, who dug into the ground with his heel, causing water to gush forth. She began collecting the water in her waterskin and was relieved of her fear and hardship. Jibril informed her that this location would one day be where her son and his father would build a house for Allah, the Ka'bah, and he gave her glad tidings of this great news.

She stayed in the area, drinking from Zamzam water, until a group of people from the tribe of Jurhum passed by. They saw a bird circling the area and said, 'This bird

---

[32] Her seeking means in no way negates her reliance (*tawakkul*) on Allah. Ibn al-Qayyim said, "True *tawhid* is only realized by seeking the means Allah has established. Neglecting them weakens the essence of reliance on Allah while abandoning them entirely is mere helplessness, which contradicts it. Genuine *tawakkul* is placing one s trust in Allah while actively pursuing what benefits both one s faith and worldly life and avoiding what harms them. Reliance on Allah must be coupled with taking action. Otherwise, it undermines divine wisdom and the *Shari ah*. Thus, one should neither confuse helplessness with *tawakkul* nor reduce *tawakkul* to passivity" (*Zad Al-Ma'ad* 3:330-331).

has found water, though this valley is not known to have water.' They sent scouts, who discovered the wellspring, returned, and informed their people. They came to Hajar and asked for permission to settle there. She agreed, saying, 'You may settle but have no right to the water.' They accepted her terms, and she was pleased with their company.

The boy Isma'il grew up among them and married from the tribe. Later, Ibrahim came to visit but found that Hajar had passed away. He asked Isma'il s wife about her condition, and she complained of hardship and poverty. Ibrahim instructed her, 'When your husband returns, convey my greetings and tell him to change the threshold of his door.' When Isma il returned, she informed him of what had happened. Isma il said, 'That was my father, and he has commanded me to separate from you.' He divorced her and married another woman.

Ibrahim returned after some time and met Isma il s new wife. When asked about her condition, she praised Allah and expressed gratitude. Ibrahim told her, 'When your husband returns, convey my greetings and tell him to keep the threshold of his door firm.' When Isma il returned, she informed him. He said, 'That was my father, and you are the threshold. He has commanded me to keep you.'

This is a narration attributed to Ibn Abbas, though it includes reports that are attributed (*marfu'*) to the Prophet ﷺ. Among them is his statement, 'Had the water been left alone, it would have become a flowing spring.' He also said that the ritual of *sa'i* originated from the striving of Isma'il's mother.

Allah legislated *sa'i* and *tawaf* during *Hajj* and *Umrah* as a reminder of this event, as well as an act of obedience, worship, and a means of drawing closer to Him. He made *tawaf* and *sa'i* essential rites of *Hajj* and *Umrah*.

This also teaches that Allah tests His servants in both ease and hardship. He tested Ibrahim by commanding him to leave Isma'il and his mother in a distant, unfamiliar land. He tested Isma'il and his mother with this as well. But Allah is All-Wise and All-Knowing in what He decrees, for His wisdom is perfect and boundless. Ultimately, the outcome was blessed for Isma'il, his mother, and all Muslims."[33]

---

[33] See: https://binbaz.org.sa/audios/2651/585

Explanation of Al-Allamah Muhammad b. Salih Al-Uthaymin

Al-Allamah Uthaymin said, "Zamzam is the wellspring of water near the Ka'bah. Its origin goes back to when Ibrahim left Hajar, the mother of Isma'il, and their son in Makkah, which at the time was completely uninhabited. There were no dwellings, no Ka'bah, and no vegetation. It was a barren valley without cultivation. Ibrahim placed a container of dates and a waterskin with them and departed, for Allah had commanded him to leave them there.

When Ibrahim was leaving, Hajar followed him and asked, 'How can you leave us here?' Then she asked, 'Did Allah command you to do this?' He replied, 'Yes.' She said, 'If Allah has commanded you, He will not abandon us.' See the strength of her faith: 'He will not abandon us.' This shows Hajar's complete trust in Allah. May Allah be pleased with her.

Her story is like that of Musa's mother. When Pharaoh oppressed the Children of Israel, killing their male infants and sparing their daughters to humiliate them, it was said that soothsayers told him that a man from the Children of Israel would rise and bring about his downfall. So, he began slaughtering their sons. Musa's mother feared for him, but Allah inspired her—not through prophecy, but through divine inspiration—to place him in a wooden box and cast him into the river. Imagine how difficult this was. A mother putting her child in a box and sending him into the water. But she had faith and trust in Allah's promise, so she obeyed. The box floated until it reached Pharaoh's household, who took the baby in. Pharaoh's wife pleaded, 'He will be a comfort to me and you. Do not kill him. Perhaps he will benefit us, or we may adopt him as a son.'

Even though Musa's mother had faith in Allah, her heart became empty with grief for her son. Yet, in Allah's wisdom, he refused to nurse from any of them whenever they brought different wet nurses for Musa. Meanwhile, Musa's sister, who had been sent to observe the situation, saw the people searching for a nurse. She said, 'Shall I direct you to a household that will care for him and be sincere to him?' And so, Allah returned Musa to his mother before he had nursed from any other woman.

Allahu Akbar! Such is the power of Allah—despite having been cast into the river, he nursed only from his mother, whom Allah returned him to.

[Returning to Hajar], when Ibrahim told her that Allah had commanded this, she said, 'Then He will not abandon me.' She remained there alone with her child in an uninhabited land. She ate dates, drank water, and nursed her son but became hungry when the dates and water ran out. And when a mother is hungry, she cannot produce milk for her child. The baby began crying and wailing. So, inspired by Allah, she searched for the nearest mountain she could climb, hoping to hear a sound or see someone.

The nearest mountain was Safa, the closest to the Ka'bah even today. She climbed Safa and listened but found no one. She descended and thought, 'I will try the other side.' The closest mountain in the other direction was Marwah, so she climbed it and listened, hoping to find someone, but no one was there. Between Safa and Marwah was a valley where floodwaters would sometimes flow. This valley was lower than the surrounding land. Whenever Hajar reached the valley, she would run swiftly to hear her child and check on him, then glance back at him as she ran. She repeated this seven times—back and forth between Safa and Marwah. After completing seven passes, she suddenly heard a sound. She said, 'Help us, if you have anything to offer!'

She saw Jibril, sent by Allah, strike the ground with his heel (or wing), and water gushed forth. This was Zamzam. Hajar quickly surrounded the water with stones to prevent it from spreading, thinking it might run out. She drank from the water and gave it to her child, and Allah relieved her distress.

At that time, an Arab tribe called Jurhum was living far away. They saw birds circling a specific area. Knowing that birds only gathered around water, they said, 'We have never known water to exist in that place.' But suspecting there might be a new spring, they followed the birds and arrived at the well of Zamzam, where they found Hajar and her child. She welcomed them, and they settled near her. Ismail grew up among them and later married from them.

Sometime later, Ibrahim returned to visit his family. He arrived at Hajar's home and met Ismail's wife. He asked her about their situation, and she complained of hardship. Ibrahim told her, 'When your husband returns, tell him to change the threshold of his door.' She agreed. Then Ismail returned, and his wife informed him of what had happened. He asked, 'Did anyone come to visit you?' as if he was skeptical that someone had come. She replied, 'Yes, an old man came with such-and-such a description. He conveyed his greetings to you and told me to tell you, 'Change the threshold of your door.'

What did Ibrahim mean by this? He was instructing Isma'il to divorce her. The reason was that she was complaining—she had spoken ill of their situation, expressing only hardship and misery. So Isma'il said, 'That was my father, and you are the threshold. Go back to your family.' He then married another woman.

Then, after some time, Ibrahim returned and visited his son Isma'il's home. He met Isma'il's wife and asked her about their situation. She praised their condition, saying, 'We are well,' and spoke positively about their circumstances. Ibrahim then said to her, 'Give my greetings to your husband and tell him to keep the threshold of his door.'

When Isma'il returned from hunting—or whatever he had been doing—he asked, 'Did anyone come to visit?' She replied, 'Yes, an old man came with such-and-such a description. He sends you his greetings and says, 'Keep the threshold of your door.'

Isma'il said, 'That was my father, and you are the threshold. He has commanded me to keep you.'

Thus, Zamzam is blessed water, both nourishing and healing. It serves as both food and drink. The Prophet ﷺ said,

$$﴿﴿مَاءُ زَمْزَمَ لِمَا شُرِبَ لَهُ﴾﴾$$

Zamzam is for whatever purpose it is drunk for."[34]

If you drink it to quench thirst, you will be satisfied. If you drink it to ease hunger, you will be nourished. Some scholars even deduced from this *hadith* that if a person drinks it for healing, they will be cured, and if they drink

[34] Collected by Ibn Majah in his *Sunan* (no. 3062) and authenticated by Al-Albani in *Sahih Sunan Ibn Majah* (no. 3062).

it for memory, they will be granted sharper recall. Whatever sincere purpose one drinks it for, it will benefit them. In any case, Zamzam is blessed water."[35]

---

[35] See https://alathar.net/home/esound/index.php?op=codevi&coid=214257

Made in the USA
Monee, IL
03 March 2025